M000101073

This Journal Belongs To:

_____

Favorite Recipes & Meals

Favorite Recipes & Meals

Start Here

Measurements

Neck

———————

Chest ———

———————

Abdomen

———————

Thighs ———

———————

Calves ———

L ——— R ———————

Upper Arms

L ——— R ———————

Waist ———————

Hips

———————

Weight ———————

BMI ———————

My Health Goals

————————————————————————
————————————————————————
————————————————————————

What Will Help Me Reach My Goals?

————————————————————————
————————————————————————
————————————————————————
————————————————————————

Tips For Success

- Do Exercise You LOVE To Do
- Add More Fruit & Veggies To Your Diet
- Love Yourself
- Get More High-Quality Sleep
- Relax More Often
- Enjoy Your Life
- Add More Gratitude To Your Life
- Keep A Food Journal
- Avoid Drama & Toxic People
- Try to Avoid Stress Whenever Possible
- Minimize Junk Food in Your Diet
- Stop Judging Yourself
- Don't Compare Yourself to Others

Most of All...Be Consistent and Keep On Going!

You CAN Do This!

Weekly Meal Planner

Monday	Tuesday	Wednesday

Thursday	Friday	Saturday

Sunday	Snack Ideas for the Week

Date_____   Hours of Sleep_____

How I'm Doing Today: Great | Good | Fair | Poor

Cups of Water: 1 2 3 4 5 6   7 8 9

In Ketosis? Yes No Ketone Levels_____

Fasting Period:

	Calories	Carbs	Protein	Fat
Breakfast				
Lunch				
Dinner				
Snacks				
Today's Totals				

Exercise Type and Duration _____

_____

_____

Date_____   Hours of Sleep_____

How I'm Doing Today: Great | Good | Fair | Poor	Cups of Water: 1 2 3 4 5 6 7 8 9
In Ketosis? Yes No Ketone Levels_____	Fasting Period:

	Calories	Carbs	Protein	Fat
Breakfast				
Lunch				
Dinner				
Snacks				
Today's Totals				

Exercise Type and Duration_____
_____
_____

Date_____   Hours of Sleep_____

How I'm Doing Today: Great | Good | Fair | Poor

Cups of Water: 1 2 3 4 5 6 7 8 9

In Ketosis? Yes No Ketone Levels_____

Fasting Period:

	Calories	Carbs	Protein	Fat
Breakfast				
Lunch				
Dinner				
Snacks				
Today's Totals				

Exercise Type and Duration _____

_____

_____

Date_____   Hours of Sleep_____

How I'm Doing Today: Great | Good | Fair | Poor	Cups of Water: 1 2 3 4 5 6 7 8 9

In Ketosis? Yes No Ketone Levels_____	Fasting Period:

	Calories	Carbs	Protein	Fat
Breakfast				
Lunch				
Dinner				
Snacks				
Today's Totals				

Exercise Type and Duration _____

_____

_____

Date_____   Hours of Sleep_____

How I'm Doing Today: Great | Good | Fair | Poor	Cups of Water: 1 2 3 4 5 6 7 8 9
In Ketosis? Yes No Ketone Levels_____	Fasting Period:

	Calories	Carbs	Protein	Fat
Breakfast				
Lunch				
Dinner				
Snacks				
Today's Totals				

Exercise Type and Duration
_____
_____
_____

Date_____   Hours of Sleep_____

How I'm Doing Today: Great | Good | Fair | Poor	Cups of Water: 1 2 3 4 5 6 7 8 9

In Ketosis? Yes No Ketone Levels_____	Fasting Period:

	Calories	Carbs	Protein	Fat
Breakfast				
Lunch				
Dinner				
Snacks				
Today's Totals				

Exercise Type and Duration _____

_____

_____

Date_____   Hours of Sleep_____

| How I'm Doing Today: |
| Great \| Good \| Fair \| Poor |

| Cups of Water: |
| 1 2 3 4 5 6 |
| 7 8 9 |

| In Ketosis? Yes   No |
| Ketone Levels_____ |

| Fasting Period: |

	Calories	Carbs	Protein	Fat
Breakfast				
Lunch				
Dinner				
Snacks				
Today's Totals				

Exercise Type and Duration _____
_____
_____

Weekly Check In

Health Victories This Week

Two Things I'm Grateful For

New Goals for Next Week

Weekly Meal Planner

Monday	Tuesday	Wednesday

Thursday	Friday	Saturday

Sunday	Snack Ideas for the Week

Date_____   Hours of Sleep_____

How I'm Doing Today: Great | Good | Fair | Poor	Cups of Water: 1 2 3 4 5 6 7 8 9
In Ketosis? Yes No Ketone Levels_____	Fasting Period:

	Calories	Carbs	Protein	Fat
Breakfast				
Lunch				
Dinner				
Snacks				
Today's Totals				

Exercise Type and Duration _____
_____
_____

Date_____   Hours of Sleep_____

How I'm Doing Today: Great | Good | Fair | Poor

Cups of Water: 1 2 3 4 5 6 7 8 9

In Ketosis? Yes No Ketone Levels_____

Fasting Period:

	Calories	Carbs	Protein	Fat
Breakfast				
Lunch				
Dinner				
Snacks				
Today's Totals				

Exercise Type and Duration _____
_____
_____

Date_____   Hours of Sleep_____

| How I'm Doing Today: | Cups of Water: |
| Great \| Good \| Fair \| Poor | 1 2 3 4 5 6
 7 8 9 |

| In Ketosis? Yes   No | Fasting Period: |
| Ketone Levels_____ | |

	Calories	Carbs	Protein	Fat
Breakfast				
Lunch				
Dinner				
Snacks				
Today's Totals				

Exercise Type and Duration _____

_____

_____

Date_____   Hours of Sleep_____

| How I'm Doing Today: |
| Great \| Good \| Fair \| Poor |

| Cups of Water: |
| 1 2 3 4 5 6 |
| 7 8 9 |

| In Ketosis? Yes No |
| Ketone Levels_____ |

| Fasting Period: |

	Calories	Carbs	Protein	Fat
Breakfast				
Lunch				
Dinner				
Snacks				
Today's Totals				

Exercise Type and Duration _____

_____

_____

Date_____   Hours of Sleep_____

How I'm Doing Today: Great | Good | Fair | Poor	Cups of Water: 1 2 3 4 5 6 7 8 9

In Ketosis? Yes No Ketone Levels_____	Fasting Period:

	Calories	Carbs	Protein	Fat
Breakfast				
Lunch				
Dinner				
Snacks				
Today's Totals				

Exercise Type and Duration _____

_____

_____

Date_____   Hours of Sleep_____

| How I'm Doing Today: |
| Great \| Good \| Fair \| Poor |

| Cups of Water: |
| 1 2 3 4 5 6 |
| 7 8 9 |

| In Ketosis? Yes No |
| Ketone Levels_____ |

| Fasting Period: |

	Calories	Carbs	Protein	Fat
Breakfast				
Lunch				
Dinner				
Snacks				
Today's Totals				

Exercise Type and Duration _____

Date_____   Hours of Sleep_____

How I'm Doing Today: Great | Good | Fair | Poor

Cups of Water: 1 2 3 4 5 6 7 8 9

In Ketosis? Yes No   Ketone Levels_____

Fasting Period:

	Calories	Carbs	Protein	Fat
Breakfast				
Lunch				
Dinner				
Snacks				
Today's Totals				

Exercise Type and Duration _____

_____

_____

Weekly Check In

Health Victories This Week

_____

_____

_____

_____

_____

_____

_____

Two Things I'm Grateful For

_____

_____

_____

_____

_____

_____

New Goals for Next Week

_____

_____

_____

_____

_____

_____

_____

Weekly Meal Planner

Monday	Tuesday	Wednesday

Thursday	Friday	Saturday

Sunday	Snack Ideas for the Week

Date_____   Hours of Sleep_____

How I'm Doing Today:	Cups of Water:
Great | Good | Fair | Poor	1 2 3 4 5 6 7 8 9

In Ketosis? Yes No	Fasting Period:
Ketone Levels_____	

	Calories	Carbs	Protein	Fat
Breakfast				
Lunch				
Dinner				
Snacks				
Today's Totals				

Exercise Type and Duration _____

_____

_____

Date_____   Hours of Sleep_____

| How I'm Doing Today: Great \| Good \| Fair \| Poor | Cups of Water: 1 2 3 4 5 6 7 8 9 |

| In Ketosis? Yes No Ketone Levels_____ | Fasting Period: |

	Calories	Carbs	Protein	Fat
Breakfast				
Lunch				
Dinner				
Snacks				
Today's Totals				

Exercise Type and Duration_____

_____

_____

Date_____   Hours of Sleep_____

How I'm Doing Today:
Great | Good | Fair | Poor

Cups of Water:
1 2 3 4 5 6
7 8 9

In Ketosis? Yes No
Ketone Levels_____

Fasting Period:

	Calories	Carbs	Protein	Fat
Breakfast				
Lunch				
Dinner				
Snacks				
Today's Totals				

Exercise Type and Duration _____

_____

_____

Date_____   Hours of Sleep_____

How I'm Doing Today:	Cups of Water:
Great | Good | Fair | Poor	1 2 3 4 5 6 7 8 9

In Ketosis? Yes No	Fasting Period:
Ketone Levels_____	

	Calories	Carbs	Protein	Fat
Breakfast				
Lunch				
Dinner				
Snacks				
Today's Totals				

Exercise Type and Duration_____
_____
_____
_____

Date_____   Hours of Sleep_____

| How I'm Doing Today: |
| Great \| Good \| Fair \| Poor |

| Cups of Water: |
| 1 2 3 4 5 6 |
| 7 8 9 |

| In Ketosis? Yes No |
| Ketone Levels_____ |

| Fasting Period: |

	Calories	Carbs	Protein	Fat
Breakfast				
Lunch				
Dinner				
Snacks				
Today's Totals				

Exercise Type and Duration_____

_____

_____

Date_____   Hours of Sleep_____

How I'm Doing Today:	Cups of Water:
Great | Good | Fair | Poor	1 2 3 4 5 6
	7 8 9

| In Ketosis? Yes No | Fasting Period: |
| Ketone Levels_____ | |

	Calories	Carbs	Protein	Fat
Breakfast				
Lunch				
Dinner				
Snacks				
Today's Totals				

Exercise Type and Duration _____

_____

_____

Date_____   Hours of Sleep_____

How I'm Doing Today:	Cups of Water:
Great | Good | Fair | Poor	1 2 3 4 5 6 7 8 9

In Ketosis? Yes No	Fasting Period:
Ketone Levels_____	

	Calories	Carbs	Protein	Fat
Breakfast				
Lunch				
Dinner				
Snacks				
Today's Totals				

Exercise Type and Duration_____

_____

_____

Weekly Check In

Health Victories This Week

_____

_____

_____

_____

_____

_____

_____

Two Things I'm Grateful For

_____

_____

_____

_____

_____

_____

New Goals for Next Week

_____

_____

_____

_____

_____

_____

_____

Weekly Meal Planner

Monday	Tuesday	Wednesday

Thursday	Friday	Saturday

Sunday	Snack Ideas for the Week

Date_____ Hours of Sleep_____

How I'm Doing Today:	Cups of Water:
Great | Good | Fair | Poor	1 2 3 4 5 6 7 8 9

In Ketosis? Yes No	Fasting Period:
Ketone Levels_____	

	Calories	Carbs	Protein	Fat
Breakfast				
Lunch				
Dinner				
Snacks				
Today's Totals				

Exercise Type and Duration _____

_____

_____

Date_____ Hours of Sleep_____

How I'm Doing Today: Great | Good | Fair | Poor	Cups of Water: 1 2 3 4 5 6 7 8 9

In Ketosis? Yes No Ketone Levels_____	Fasting Period:

	Calories	Carbs	Protein	Fat
Breakfast				
Lunch				
Dinner				
Snacks				
Today's Totals				

Exercise Type and Duration_____

_____

_____

Date_____   Hours of Sleep_____

How I'm Doing Today: Great | Good | Fair | Poor

Cups of Water: 1 2 3 4 5 6 7 8 9

In Ketosis? Yes No Ketone Levels_____

Fasting Period:

	Calories	Carbs	Protein	Fat
Breakfast				
Lunch				
Dinner				
Snacks				
Today's Totals				

Exercise Type and Duration _____

_____

_____

Date_____   Hours of Sleep_____

How I'm Doing Today: Great | Good | Fair | Poor	Cups of Water: 1 2 3 4 5 6 7 8 9

In Ketosis? Yes No Ketone Levels_____	Fasting Period:

	Calories	Carbs	Protein	Fat
Breakfast				
Lunch				
Dinner				
Snacks				
Today's Totals				

Exercise Type and Duration_____
_____
_____

Date_____   Hours of Sleep_____

How I'm Doing Today: Great | Good | Fair | Poor	Cups of Water: 1 2 3 4 5 6 7 8 9
In Ketosis? Yes No Ketone Levels_____	Fasting Period:

	Calories	Carbs	Protein	Fat
Breakfast				
Lunch				
Dinner				
Snacks				
Today's Totals				

Exercise Type and Duration _____
_____
_____

Date_____ Hours of Sleep_____

How I'm Doing Today: Great | Good | Fair | Poor	Cups of Water: 1 2 3 4 5 6 7 8 9

In Ketosis? Yes No Ketone Levels_____	Fasting Period:

	Calories	Carbs	Protein	Fat
Breakfast				
Lunch				
Dinner				
Snacks				
Today's Totals				

Exercise Type and Duration _____

_____

_____

Date_____   Hours of Sleep_____

How I'm Doing Today: Great | Good | Fair | Poor

Cups of Water: 1 2 3 4 5 6   7 8 9

In Ketosis? Yes No Ketone Levels_____

Fasting Period:

	Calories	Carbs	Protein	Fat
Breakfast				
Lunch				
Dinner				
Snacks				
Today's Totals				

Exercise Type and Duration_____

_____

_____

Weekly Check In

Health Victories This Week

_____
_____
_____
_____
_____
_____
_____
_____

Two Things I'm Grateful For

_____
_____
_____
_____
_____
_____
_____

New Goals for Next Week

_____
_____
_____
_____
_____
_____
_____

Weekly Meal Planner

Monday	Tuesday	Wednesday

Thursday	Friday	Saturday

Sunday	Snack Ideas for the Week

Date_____   Hours of Sleep_____

How I'm Doing Today: Great | Good | Fair | Poor

Cups of Water: 1 2 3 4 5 6   7 8 9

In Ketosis? Yes No Ketone Levels_____

Fasting Period:

	Calories	Carbs	Protein	Fat
Breakfast				
Lunch				
Dinner				
Snacks				
Today's Totals				

Exercise Type and Duration _____

_____

_____

Date_____   Hours of Sleep_____

How I'm Doing Today: Great | Good | Fair | Poor	Cups of Water: 1 2 3 4 5 6 7 8 9
In Ketosis? Yes No Ketone Levels_____	Fasting Period:

	Calories	Carbs	Protein	Fat
Breakfast				
Lunch				
Dinner				
Snacks				
Today's Totals				

Exercise Type and Duration _____

_____

_____

30-Day Check In

Measurements

Neck

_____

Chest _____

_____

Abdomen

_____

Thighs

_____

Calves

L _____ R _____

Upper Arms

L _____ R _____

Waist _____

Hips

_____

_____

Weight _____

BMI _____

How Are Things Going So Far?

_____

_____

_____

What's Working Well For Me Right Now?

_____

_____

_____

_____

Date_____   Hours of Sleep_____

How I'm Doing Today: Great | Good | Fair | Poor

Cups of Water: 1 2 3 4 5 6 7 8 9

In Ketosis? Yes No Ketone Levels_____

Fasting Period:

	Calories	Carbs	Protein	Fat
Breakfast				
Lunch				
Dinner				
Snacks				
Today's Totals				

Exercise Type and Duration _____

_____

_____

Date_____   Hours of Sleep_____

How I'm Doing Today: Great | Good | Fair | Poor

Cups of Water: 1 2 3 4 5 6 7 8 9

In Ketosis? Yes No Ketone Levels_____

Fasting Period:

	Calories	Carbs	Protein	Fat
Breakfast				
Lunch				
Dinner				
Snacks				
Today's Totals				

Exercise Type and Duration _____

_____

_____

Date_____   Hours of Sleep_____

| How I'm Doing Today: |
| Great \| Good \| Fair \| Poor |

| Cups of Water: |
| 1 2 3 4 5 6 |
| 7 8 9 |

| In Ketosis? Yes No |
| Ketone Levels_____ |

| Fasting Period: |

	Calories	Carbs	Protein	Fat
Breakfast				
Lunch				
Dinner				
Snacks				
Today's Totals				

Exercise Type and Duration _____

_____

_____

Date_____   Hours of Sleep_____

| How I'm Doing Today:
Great \| Good \| Fair \| Poor | Cups of Water:
1 2 3 4 5 6
7 8 9 |

| In Ketosis? Yes No
Ketone Levels_____ | Fasting Period: |

	Calories	Carbs	Protein	Fat
Breakfast				
Lunch				
Dinner				
Snacks				
Today's Totals				

Exercise Type and Duration _____

_____

Date_____   Hours of Sleep_____

How I'm Doing Today: Great | Good | Fair | Poor	Cups of Water: 1 2 3 4 5 6 7 8 9

In Ketosis? Yes No Ketone Levels_____	Fasting Period:

	Calories	Carbs	Protein	Fat
Breakfast				
Lunch				
Dinner				
Snacks				
Today's Totals				

Exercise Type and Duration _____

_____

_____

Weekly Check In

Health Victories This Week

_____

_____

_____

_____

_____

_____

_____

_____

Two Things I'm Grateful For

_____

_____

_____

_____

_____

_____

_____

New Goals for Next Week

_____

_____

_____

_____

_____

_____

_____

_____

Weekly Meal Planner

Monday	Tuesday	Wednesday

Thursday	Friday	Saturday

Sunday	Snack Ideas for the Week

Date_____   Hours of Sleep_____

How I'm Doing Today: Great | Good | Fair | Poor	Cups of Water: 1 2 3 4 5 6 7 8 9

In Ketosis? Yes No Ketone Levels_____	Fasting Period:

	Calories	Carbs	Protein	Fat
Breakfast				
Lunch				
Dinner				
Snacks				
Today's Totals				

Exercise Type and Duration _____

_____

_____

Date_____   Hours of Sleep_____

How I'm Doing Today:	Cups of Water:
Great | Good | Fair | Poor	1 2 3 4 5 6 7 8 9

In Ketosis? Yes No	Fasting Period:
Ketone Levels_____	

	Calories	Carbs	Protein	Fat
Breakfast				
Lunch				
Dinner				
Snacks				
Today's Totals				

Exercise Type and Duration _____

_____

_____

Date_____   Hours of Sleep_____

How I'm Doing Today: Great | Good | Fair | Poor	Cups of Water: 1 2 3 4 5 6 7 8 9
In Ketosis? Yes No Ketone Levels_____	Fasting Period:

	Calories	Carbs	Protein	Fat
Breakfast				
Lunch				
Dinner				
Snacks				
Today's Totals				

Exercise Type and Duration _____

_____

_____

Date_____   Hours of Sleep_____

How I'm Doing Today: Great | Good | Fair | Poor	Cups of Water: 1 2 3 4 5 6 7 8 9

In Ketosis? Yes No Ketone Levels_____	Fasting Period:

	Calories	Carbs	Protein	Fat
Breakfast				
Lunch				
Dinner				
Snacks				
Today's Totals				

Exercise Type and Duration _____

_____

_____

Date_____ Hours of Sleep_____

How I'm Doing Today: Great | Good | Fair | Poor	Cups of Water: 1 2 3 4 5 6 7 8 9

In Ketosis? Yes No Ketone Levels_____	Fasting Period:

	Calories	Carbs	Protein	Fat
Breakfast				
Lunch				
Dinner				
Snacks				
Today's Totals				

Exercise Type and Duration_____

_____

_____

Date_____ Hours of Sleep_____

How I'm Doing Today: Great | Good | Fair | Poor	Cups of Water: 1 2 3 4 5 6 7 8 9
In Ketosis? Yes No Ketone Levels_____	Fasting Period:

	Calories	Carbs	Protein	Fat
Breakfast				
Lunch				
Dinner				
Snacks				
Today's Totals				

Exercise Type and Duration _____

_____

_____

Date_____   Hours of Sleep_____

How I'm Doing Today: Great | Good | Fair | Poor

Cups of Water: 1 2 3 4 5 6   7 8 9

In Ketosis? Yes No   Ketone Levels_____

Fasting Period:

	Calories	Carbs	Protein	Fat
Breakfast				
Lunch				
Dinner				
Snacks				
Today's Totals				

Exercise Type and Duration_____

_____

_____

Weekly Check In

Health Victories This Week

_____
_____
_____
_____
_____
_____
_____
_____

Two Things I'm Grateful For

_____
_____
_____
_____
_____
_____
_____

New Goals for Next Week

_____
_____
_____
_____
_____
_____
_____
_____

Weekly Meal Planner

Monday	Tuesday	Wednesday

Thursday	Friday	Saturday

Sunday	Snack Ideas for the Week

Date_____   Hours of Sleep_____

How I'm Doing Today: Great | Good | Fair | Poor	Cups of Water: 1 2 3 4 5 6 7 8 9

In Ketosis? Yes No Ketone Levels_____	Fasting Period:

	Calories	Carbs	Protein	Fat
Breakfast				
Lunch				
Dinner				
Snacks				
Today's Totals				

Exercise Type and Duration_____

_____

_____

Date_____   Hours of Sleep_____

How I'm Doing Today: Great | Good | Fair | Poor	Cups of Water: 1 2 3 4 5 6 7 8 9

In Ketosis? Yes No Ketone Levels_____	Fasting Period:

	Calories	Carbs	Protein	Fat
Breakfast				
Lunch				
Dinner				
Snacks				
Today's Totals				

Exercise Type and Duration _____
_____
_____

Date_____   Hours of Sleep_____

How I'm Doing Today: Great | Good | Fair | Poor	Cups of Water: 1 2 3 4 5 6 7 8 9
In Ketosis? Yes No Ketone Levels_____	Fasting Period:

	Calories	Carbs	Protein	Fat
Breakfast				
Lunch				
Dinner				
Snacks				
Today's Totals				

Exercise Type and Duration _____

_____

_____

Date_____   Hours of Sleep_____

How I'm Doing Today: Great | Good | Fair | Poor

Cups of Water: 1 2 3 4 5 6 7 8 9

In Ketosis? Yes No Ketone Levels_____

Fasting Period:

	Calories	Carbs	Protein	Fat
Breakfast				
Lunch				
Dinner				
Snacks				
Today's Totals				

Exercise Type and Duration _____

_____

_____

Date_____ Hours of Sleep_____

| How I'm Doing Today: Great \| Good \| Fair \| Poor | Cups of Water: 1 2 3 4 5 6 7 8 9 |

| In Ketosis? Yes No Ketone Levels_____ | Fasting Period: |

	Calories	Carbs	Protein	Fat
Breakfast				
Lunch				
Dinner				
Snacks				
Today's Totals				

Exercise Type and Duration
_____
_____

Date_____ Hours of Sleep_____

| How I'm Doing Today: Great \| Good \| Fair \| Poor | Cups of Water: 1 2 3 4 5 6 7 8 9 |

| In Ketosis? Yes No Ketone Levels_____ | Fasting Period: |

	Calories	Carbs	Protein	Fat
Breakfast				
Lunch				
Dinner				
Snacks				
Today's Totals				

Exercise Type and Duration _____

Date_____ Hours of Sleep_____

How I'm Doing Today: Great | Good | Fair | Poor	Cups of Water: 1 2 3 4 5 6 7 8 9

In Ketosis? Yes No Ketone Levels_____	Fasting Period:

	Calories	Carbs	Protein	Fat
Breakfast				
Lunch				
Dinner				
Snacks				
Today's Totals				

Exercise Type and Duration_____

_____

_____

Weekly Check In

Health Victories This Week
_____
_____
_____
_____
_____
_____
_____

Two Things I'm Grateful For
_____
_____
_____
_____
_____
_____

New Goals for Next Week
_____
_____
_____
_____
_____
_____
_____

Weekly Meal Planner

Monday	Tuesday	Wednesday

Thursday	Friday	Saturday

Sunday	Snack Ideas for the Week

Date_____   Hours of Sleep_____

How I'm Doing Today: Great | Good | Fair | Poor	Cups of Water: 1 2 3 4 5 6 7 8 9

In Ketosis? Yes No Ketone Levels_____	Fasting Period:

	Calories	Carbs	Protein	Fat
Breakfast				
Lunch				
Dinner				
Snacks				
Today's Totals				

Exercise Type and Duration _____
_____
_____

Date_____   Hours of Sleep_____

How I'm Doing Today: Great | Good | Fair | Poor	Cups of Water: 1 2 3 4 5 6 7 8 9
In Ketosis? Yes No Ketone Levels_____	Fasting Period:

	Calories	Carbs	Protein	Fat
Breakfast				
Lunch				
Dinner				
Snacks				
Today's Totals				

Exercise Type and Duration
_____
_____

Date_____   Hours of Sleep_____

| How I'm Doing Today: Great \| Good \| Fair \| Poor | Cups of Water: 1 2 3 4 5 6 7 8 9 |

| In Ketosis? Yes No Ketone Levels_____ | Fasting Period: |

	Calories	Carbs	Protein	Fat
Breakfast				
Lunch				
Dinner				
Snacks				
Today's Totals				

Exercise Type and Duration _____

_____

_____

Date_____   Hours of Sleep_____

How I'm Doing Today: Great | Good | Fair | Poor

Cups of Water: 1 2 3 4 5 6 7 8 9

In Ketosis? Yes No Ketone Levels_____

Fasting Period:

	Calories	Carbs	Protein	Fat
Breakfast				
Lunch				
Dinner				
Snacks				
Today's Totals				

Exercise Type and Duration _____

_____

_____

Date_____   Hours of Sleep_____

How I'm Doing Today: Great | Good | Fair | Poor

Cups of Water: 1 2 3 4 5 6   7 8 9

In Ketosis? Yes No Ketone Levels_____

Fasting Period:

	Calories	Carbs	Protein	Fat
Breakfast				
Lunch				
Dinner				
Snacks				
Today's Totals				

Exercise Type and Duration _____

_____

_____

Date_____   Hours of Sleep_____

How I'm Doing Today: Great | Good | Fair | Poor	Cups of Water: 1 2 3 4 5 6 7 8 9

In Ketosis? Yes No Ketone Levels_____	Fasting Period:

	Calories	Carbs	Protein	Fat
Breakfast				
Lunch				
Dinner				
Snacks				
Today's Totals				

Exercise Type and Duration_____

_____

_____

Date_____   Hours of Sleep_____

How I'm Doing Today: Great | Good | Fair | Poor	Cups of Water: 1 2 3 4 5 6 7 8 9

In Ketosis? Yes No Ketone Levels_____	Fasting Period:

	Calories	Carbs	Protein	Fat
Breakfast				
Lunch				
Dinner				
Snacks				
Today's Totals				

Exercise Type and Duration _____

_____

_____

Weekly Check In

Health Victories This Week

_____

_____

_____

_____

_____

_____

_____

Two Things I'm Grateful For

_____

_____

_____

_____

_____

_____

_____

New Goals for Next Week

_____

_____

_____

_____

_____

_____

_____

Weekly Meal Planner

Monday	Tuesday	Wednesday

Thursday	Friday	Saturday

Sunday	Snack Ideas for the Week

Date_____   Hours of Sleep_____

| How I'm Doing Today: |
| Great \| Good \| Fair \| Poor |

| Cups of Water: |
| 1 2 3 4 5 6 |
| 7 8 9 |

| In Ketosis? Yes No |
| Ketone Levels_____ |

| Fasting Period: |

	Calories	Carbs	Protein	Fat
Breakfast				
Lunch				
Dinner				
Snacks				
Today's Totals				

Exercise Type and Duration _____
_____
_____

Date_____   Hours of Sleep_____

How I'm Doing Today: Great | Good | Fair | Poor	Cups of Water: 1 2 3 4 5 6 7 8 9

In Ketosis? Yes No Ketone Levels_____	Fasting Period:

	Calories	Carbs	Protein	Fat
Breakfast				
Lunch				
Dinner				
Snacks				
Today's Totals				

Exercise Type and Duration _____

_____

_____

Date_____   Hours of Sleep_____

| How I'm Doing Today: |
| Great \| Good \| Fair \| Poor |

| Cups of Water: |
| 1 2 3 4 5 6 |
| 7 8 9 |

| In Ketosis? Yes No |
| Ketone Levels_____ |

| Fasting Period: |

	Calories	Carbs	Protein	Fat
Breakfast				
Lunch				
Dinner				
Snacks				
Today's Totals				

Exercise Type and Duration
_____
_____
_____

Date_____   Hours of Sleep_____

How I'm Doing Today: Great | Good | Fair | Poor

Cups of Water: 1 2 3 4 5 6   7 8 9

In Ketosis? Yes No   Ketone Levels_____

Fasting Period:

	Calories	Carbs	Protein	Fat
Breakfast				
Lunch				
Dinner				
Snacks				
Today's Totals				

Exercise Type and Duration _____

_____

_____

60-Day Check In

Measurements

Neck

_____

Chest _____

_____

Abdomen

_____

Thighs

_____

Calves

L _____   R _____

Upper Arms

L _____   R _____

Waist _____

Hips

_____

Weight _____

BMI _____

How Are Things Going So Far?

_____
_____
_____

What Will I Keep Doing? What Will I Change?

_____
_____
_____
_____

Date_____   Hours of Sleep_____

How I'm Doing Today:
Great | Good | Fair | Poor

Cups of Water:
1 2 3 4 5 6
7 8 9

| In Ketosis? Yes No |
| Ketone Levels_____ |

Fasting Period:

	Calories	Carbs	Protein	Fat
Breakfast				
Lunch				
Dinner				
Snacks				
Today's Totals				

Exercise Type and Duration _____
_____
_____

Date_____   Hours of Sleep_____

How I'm Doing Today: Great	Good	Fair	Poor

Cups of Water: 1 2 3 4 5 6 7 8 9

In Ketosis? Yes No Ketone Levels_____

Fasting Period:

	Calories	Carbs	Protein	Fat
Breakfast				
Lunch				
Dinner				
Snacks				
Today's Totals				

Exercise Type and Duration _____

_____

_____

Date_____   Hours of Sleep_____

How I'm Doing Today: Great	Good	Fair	Poor

Cups of Water: 1 2 3 4 5 6 7 8 9

In Ketosis? Yes No Ketone Levels_____

Fasting Period:

	Calories	Carbs	Protein	Fat
Breakfast				
Lunch				
Dinner				
Snacks				
Today's Totals				

Exercise Type and Duration_____

_____

_____

Weekly Check In

Health Victories This Week

_____

_____

_____

_____

_____

_____

Two Things I'm Grateful For

_____

_____

_____

_____

_____

_____

New Goals for Next Week

_____

_____

_____

_____

_____

_____

_____

Weekly Meal Planner

Monday	Tuesday	Wednesday

Thursday	Friday	Saturday

Sunday	Snack Ideas for the Week

Date_____   Hours of Sleep_____

How I'm Doing Today: Great | Good | Fair | Poor

Cups of Water: 1 2 3 4 5 6 7 8 9

In Ketosis? Yes No Ketone Levels_____

Fasting Period:

	Calories	Carbs	Protein	Fat
Breakfast				
Lunch				
Dinner				
Snacks				
Today's Totals				

Exercise Type and Duration_____

_____

_____

Date_____   Hours of Sleep_____

How I'm Doing Today: Great | Good | Fair | Poor

Cups of Water: 1 2 3 4 5 6   7 8 9

In Ketosis? Yes No Ketone Levels_____

Fasting Period:

	Calories	Carbs	Protein	Fat
Breakfast				
Lunch				
Dinner				
Snacks				
Today's Totals				

Exercise Type and Duration_____

_____

_____

Date_____   Hours of Sleep_____

How I'm Doing Today: Great | Good | Fair | Poor	Cups of Water: 1 2 3 4 5 6 7 8 9

In Ketosis? Yes No Ketone Levels_____	Fasting Period:

	Calories	Carbs	Protein	Fat
Breakfast				
Lunch				
Dinner				
Snacks				
Today's Totals				

Exercise Type and Duration _____

_____

_____

Date_____   Hours of Sleep_____

How I'm Doing Today: Great | Good | Fair | Poor

Cups of Water: 1 2 3 4 5 6 7 8 9

In Ketosis? Yes No Ketone Levels_____

Fasting Period:

	Calories	Carbs	Protein	Fat
Breakfast				
Lunch				
Dinner				
Snacks				
Today's Totals				

Exercise Type and Duration_____

Date_____   Hours of Sleep_____

How I'm Doing Today: Great | Good | Fair | Poor

Cups of Water: 1 2 3 4 5 6 7 8 9

In Ketosis? Yes No Ketone Levels_____

Fasting Period:

	Calories	Carbs	Protein	Fat
Breakfast				
Lunch				
Dinner				
Snacks				
Today's Totals				

Exercise Type and Duration _____

_____

_____

Date_____   Hours of Sleep_____

How I'm Doing Today: Great | Good | Fair | Poor	Cups of Water: 1 2 3 4 5 6 7 8 9

In Ketosis? Yes No Ketone Levels_____	Fasting Period:

	Calories	Carbs	Protein	Fat
Breakfast				
Lunch				
Dinner				
Snacks				
Today's Totals				

Exercise Type and Duration _____
_____
_____

Date_____   Hours of Sleep_____

How I'm Doing Today: Great | Good | Fair | Poor

Cups of Water: 1 2 3 4 5 6 7 8 9

In Ketosis? Yes No Ketone Levels_____

Fasting Period:

	Calories	Carbs	Protein	Fat
Breakfast				
Lunch				
Dinner				
Snacks				
Today's Totals				

Exercise Type and Duration_____

_____

_____

Weekly Check In

Health Victories This Week

_____
_____
_____
_____
_____
_____
_____

Two Things I'm Grateful For

_____
_____
_____
_____
_____
_____
_____

New Goals for Next Week

_____
_____
_____
_____
_____
_____
_____

Weekly Meal Planner

Monday	Tuesday	Wednesday

Thursday	Friday	Saturday

Sunday	Snack Ideas for the Week

Date_____   Hours of Sleep_____

How I'm Doing Today: Great | Good | Fair | Poor	Cups of Water: 1 2 3 4 5 6 7 8 9
In Ketosis? Yes No Ketone Levels_____	Fasting Period:

	Calories	Carbs	Protein	Fat
Breakfast				
Lunch				
Dinner				
Snacks				
Today's Totals				

Exercise Type and Duration _____

_____

Date_____   Hours of Sleep_____

How I'm Doing Today: Great | Good | Fair | Poor	Cups of Water: 1 2 3 4 5 6 7 8 9

In Ketosis? Yes No Ketone Levels_____	Fasting Period:

	Calories	Carbs	Protein	Fat
Breakfast				
Lunch				
Dinner				
Snacks				
Today's Totals				

Exercise Type and Duration _____

_____

_____

Date_____   Hours of Sleep_____

How I'm Doing Today: Great | Good | Fair | Poor	Cups of Water: 1 2 3 4 5 6 7 8 9
In Ketosis? Yes No Ketone Levels_____	Fasting Period:

	Calories	Carbs	Protein	Fat
Breakfast				
Lunch				
Dinner				
Snacks				
Today's Totals				

Exercise Type and Duration _____

_____

_____

Date_____   Hours of Sleep_____

How I'm Doing Today:	Cups of Water:
Great | Good | Fair | Poor	1 2 3 4 5 6
	7 8 9

| In Ketosis? Yes No | Fasting Period: |
| Ketone Levels_____ | |

	Calories	Carbs	Protein	Fat
Breakfast				
Lunch				
Dinner				
Snacks				
Today's Totals				

Exercise Type and Duration _____

_____
_____
_____

Date_____   Hours of Sleep_____

How I'm Doing Today: Great | Good | Fair | Poor	Cups of Water: 1 2 3 4 5 6 7 8 9
In Ketosis? Yes No Ketone Levels_____	Fasting Period:

	Calories	Carbs	Protein	Fat
Breakfast				
Lunch				
Dinner				
Snacks				
Today's Totals				

Exercise Type and Duration _____

_____

_____

Date_____   Hours of Sleep_____

How I'm Doing Today: Great | Good | Fair | Poor	Cups of Water: 1 2 3 4 5 6 7 8 9
In Ketosis? Yes No Ketone Levels_____	Fasting Period:

	Calories	Carbs	Protein	Fat
Breakfast				
Lunch				
Dinner				
Snacks				
Today's Totals				

Exercise Type and Duration _____

_____

_____

Date_____   Hours of Sleep_____

How I'm Doing Today: Great | Good | Fair | Poor	Cups of Water: 1 2 3 4 5 6 7 8 9

In Ketosis? Yes No Ketone Levels_____	Fasting Period:

	Calories	Carbs	Protein	Fat
Breakfast				
Lunch				
Dinner				
Snacks				
Today's Totals				

Exercise Type and Duration _____

_____

_____

Weekly Check In

Health Victories This Week

_____

_____

_____

_____

_____

_____

_____

Two Things I'm Grateful For

_____

_____

_____

_____

_____

_____

New Goals for Next Week

_____

_____

_____

_____

_____

_____

_____

Weekly Meal Planner

Monday

Tuesday

Wednesday

Thursday

Friday

Saturday

Sunday

Snack Ideas for the Week

Date_____   Hours of Sleep_____

How I'm Doing Today: Great | Good | Fair | Poor	Cups of Water: 1 2 3 4 5 6 7 8 9
In Ketosis? Yes No Ketone Levels_____	Fasting Period:

	Calories	Carbs	Protein	Fat
Breakfast				
Lunch				
Dinner				
Snacks				
Today's Totals				

Exercise Type and Duration_____

_____

_____

Date_____   Hours of Sleep_____

| How I'm Doing Today: Great \| Good \| Fair \| Poor | Cups of Water: 1 2 3 4 5 6   7 8 9 |

| In Ketosis? Yes No Ketone Levels_____ | Fasting Period: |

	Calories	Carbs	Protein	Fat
Breakfast				
Lunch				
Dinner				
Snacks				
Today's Totals				

Exercise Type and Duration _____

Date_____   Hours of Sleep_____

How I'm Doing Today: Great | Good | Fair | Poor

Cups of Water: 1 2 3 4 5 6 7 8 9

In Ketosis? Yes No Ketone Levels_____

Fasting Period:

	Calories	Carbs	Protein	Fat
Breakfast				
Lunch				
Dinner				
Snacks				
Today's Totals				

Exercise Type and Duration _____
_____
_____

Date_____   Hours of Sleep_____

How I'm Doing Today: Great | Good | Fair | Poor

Cups of Water: 1 2 3 4 5 6   7 8 9

In Ketosis? Yes No   Ketone Levels_____

Fasting Period:

	Calories	Carbs	Protein	Fat
Breakfast				
Lunch				
Dinner				
Snacks				
Today's Totals				

Exercise Type and Duration _____

_____

_____

Date_____   Hours of Sleep_____

| How I'm Doing Today: Great \| Good \| Fair \| Poor | Cups of Water: 1 2 3 4 5 6 7 8 9 |

| In Ketosis? Yes No Ketone Levels_____ | Fasting Period: |

	Calories	Carbs	Protein	Fat
Breakfast				
Lunch				
Dinner				
Snacks				
Today's Totals				

Exercise Type and Duration _____

_____

_____

Date_____   Hours of Sleep_____

How I'm Doing Today: Great | Good | Fair | Poor	Cups of Water: 1 2 3 4 5 6 7 8 9

In Ketosis? Yes No Ketone Levels_____	Fasting Period:

	Calories	Carbs	Protein	Fat
Breakfast				
Lunch				
Dinner				
Snacks				
Today's Totals				

Exercise Type and Duration_____

_____

_____

Date_____   Hours of Sleep_____

How I'm Doing Today: Great | Good | Fair | Poor

Cups of Water: 1 2 3 4 5 6 7 8 9

In Ketosis? Yes No Ketone Levels_____

Fasting Period:

	Calories	Carbs	Protein	Fat
Breakfast				
Lunch				
Dinner				
Snacks				
Today's Totals				

Exercise Type and Duration _____

_____

_____

Weekly Check In

Health Victories This Week

_____
_____
_____
_____
_____
_____
_____
_____

Two Things I'm Grateful For

_____
_____
_____
_____
_____
_____
_____
_____

New Goals for Next Week

_____
_____
_____
_____
_____
_____
_____
_____

Weekly Meal Planner

Monday	Tuesday	Wednesday

Thursday	Friday	Saturday

Sunday	Snack Ideas for the Week

Date_____   Hours of Sleep_____

How I'm Doing Today: Great | Good | Fair | Poor

Cups of Water: 1 2 3 4 5 6   7 8 9

In Ketosis? Yes No   Ketone Levels_____

Fasting Period:

	Calories	Carbs	Protein	Fat
Breakfast				
Lunch				
Dinner				
Snacks				
Today's Totals				

Exercise Type and Duration _____
_____
_____

Date_____   Hours of Sleep_____

How I'm Doing Today: Great | Good | Fair | Poor

Cups of Water: 1 2 3 4 5 6 7 8 9

In Ketosis? Yes No   Ketone Levels_____

Fasting Period:

	Calories	Carbs	Protein	Fat
Breakfast				
Lunch				
Dinner				
Snacks				
Today's Totals				

Exercise Type and Duration _____
_____
_____

Date_____   Hours of Sleep_____

How I'm Doing Today: Great | Good | Fair | Poor	Cups of Water: 1 2 3 4 5 6 7 8 9

In Ketosis? Yes No Ketone Levels_____	Fasting Period:

	Calories	Carbs	Protein	Fat
Breakfast				
Lunch				
Dinner				
Snacks				
Today's Totals				

Exercise Type and Duration _____

_____

_____

Date_____   Hours of Sleep_____

How I'm Doing Today: Great | Good | Fair | Poor

Cups of Water: 1 2 3 4 5 6 7 8 9

In Ketosis? Yes No Ketone Levels_____

Fasting Period:

	Calories	Carbs	Protein	Fat
Breakfast				
Lunch				
Dinner				
Snacks				
Today's Totals				

Exercise Type and Duration _____

_____

_____

Date_____   Hours of Sleep_____

How I'm Doing Today: Great | Good | Fair | Poor	Cups of Water: 1 2 3 4 5 6 7 8 9

In Ketosis? Yes No	Fasting Period:

Ketone Levels_____

	Calories	Carbs	Protein	Fat
Breakfast				
Lunch				
Dinner				
Snacks				
Today's Totals				

Exercise Type and Duration_____

_____

_____

Date_____   Hours of Sleep_____

How I'm Doing Today: Great | Good | Fair | Poor	Cups of Water: 1 2 3 4 5 6 7 8 9
In Ketosis? Yes No Ketone Levels_____	Fasting Period:

	Calories	Carbs	Protein	Fat
Breakfast				
Lunch				
Dinner				
Snacks				
Today's Totals				

Exercise Type and Duration _____

_____

_____

Weekly Check In

Health Victories This Week

_____
_____
_____
_____
_____
_____
_____

Two Things I'm Grateful For

_____
_____
_____
_____
_____
_____
_____

New Goals for Next Week

_____
_____
_____
_____
_____
_____
_____

End Here

Measurements

Neck

_____

Chest

_____

Abdomen

_____

Thighs

_____

Calves

L _____ R _____

Upper Arms

L _____ R _____

Waist

_____

Hips

_____

Weight _____

BMI _____

Health Improvements I Experienced

_____
_____
_____

Good Habits I Can Continue to Practice

_____
_____
_____
_____

Recipe Name_____

Where I Got It_____

Servings_____ Calories_____ Carbs_____ Protein_____ Fat_____

Ingredients

_____
_____
_____
_____
_____
_____
_____
_____
_____
_____

Directions

_____
_____
_____
_____
_____
_____
_____
_____
_____
_____
_____
_____
_____
_____

Recipe Name_____

*Where I Got It*_____

*Servings*_____ *Calories*_____ *Carbs*_____ *Protein*_____ *Fat*_____

Ingredients

_____
_____
_____
_____
_____
_____
_____
_____
_____
_____
_____

Directions

_____
_____
_____
_____
_____
_____
_____
_____
_____
_____
_____
_____
_____
_____
_____

Recipe Name_____

Where I Got It_____

Servings_____ Calories_____ Carbs_____ Protein_____ Fat_____

Ingredients

_____
_____
_____
_____
_____
_____
_____
_____
_____
_____
_____

Directions

_____
_____
_____
_____
_____
_____
_____
_____
_____
_____
_____
_____
_____
_____
_____
_____

Recipe Name_____

Where I Got It_____

Servings_____ Calories_____ Carbs_____ Protein_____ Fat_____

Ingredients

_____
_____
_____
_____
_____
_____
_____
_____
_____
_____

Directions

_____
_____
_____
_____
_____
_____
_____
_____
_____
_____
_____
_____
_____
_____
_____

Recipe Name_____

Where I Got It_____

Servings_____ Calories_____ Carbs_____ Protein_____ Fat_____

Ingredients

_____
_____
_____
_____
_____
_____
_____
_____
_____
_____
_____

Directions

_____
_____
_____
_____
_____
_____
_____
_____
_____
_____
_____
_____
_____
_____
_____
_____

Recipe Name_____

Where I Got It_____

Servings_____ Calories_____ Carbs_____ Protein_____ Fat_____

Ingredients

_____
_____
_____
_____
_____
_____
_____
_____
_____
_____

Directions

_____
_____
_____
_____
_____
_____
_____
_____
_____
_____
_____
_____
_____
_____
_____

Recipe Name_____

Where I Got It_____

Servings_____ Calories_____ Carbs_____ Protein_____ Fat_____

Ingredients

_____
_____
_____
_____
_____
_____
_____
_____
_____
_____
_____

Directions

_____
_____
_____
_____
_____
_____
_____
_____
_____
_____
_____
_____
_____
_____
_____
_____

Recipe Name_____

Where I Got It_____

Servings_____ Calories_____ Carbs_____ Protein_____ Fat_____

Ingredients

_____
_____
_____
_____
_____
_____
_____
_____
_____
_____
_____
_____

Directions

_____
_____
_____
_____
_____
_____
_____
_____
_____
_____
_____
_____
_____
_____
_____
_____

Recipe Name_____

Where I Got It_____

Servings_____ Calories_____ Carbs_____ Protein_____ Fat_____

Ingredients

_____
_____
_____
_____
_____
_____
_____
_____
_____
_____

Directions

_____
_____
_____
_____
_____
_____
_____
_____
_____
_____
_____
_____
_____
_____
_____
_____

Recipe Name_____

Where I Got It_____

Servings_____ Calories_____ Carbs_____ Protein_____ Fat_____

Ingredients

_____
_____
_____
_____
_____
_____
_____
_____
_____
_____
_____

Directions

_____
_____
_____
_____
_____
_____
_____
_____
_____
_____
_____
_____
_____
_____
_____
_____

Recipe Name_____

Where I Got It_____

Servings_____ Calories_____ Carbs_____ Protein_____ Fat_____

Ingredients

_____
_____
_____
_____
_____
_____
_____
_____
_____
_____

Directions

_____
_____
_____
_____
_____
_____
_____
_____
_____
_____
_____
_____
_____
_____
_____

Recipe Name_____

Where I Got It_____

Servings_____ Calories_____ Carbs_____ Protein_____ Fat_____

Ingredients

_____
_____
_____
_____
_____
_____
_____
_____
_____
_____

Directions

_____
_____
_____
_____
_____
_____
_____
_____
_____
_____
_____
_____
_____
_____
_____
_____

Recipe Name_____

*Where I Got It*_____

Servings_____ Calories_____ Carbs_____ Protein_____ Fat_____

Ingredients

_____
_____
_____
_____
_____
_____
_____
_____
_____

Directions

_____
_____
_____
_____
_____
_____
_____
_____
_____
_____
_____
_____
_____
_____
_____

Recipe Name_____

*Where I Got It*_____

*Servings*_____ *Calories*_____ *Carbs*_____ *Protein*_____ *Fat*_____

Ingredients

_____
_____
_____
_____
_____
_____
_____
_____
_____
_____
_____

Directions

_____
_____
_____
_____
_____
_____
_____
_____
_____
_____
_____
_____
_____
_____
_____
_____

Recipe Name_____

Where I Got It_____

Servings_____ Calories_____ Carbs_____ Protein_____ Fat_____

Ingredients

_____
_____
_____
_____
_____
_____
_____
_____
_____
_____

Directions

_____
_____
_____
_____
_____
_____
_____
_____
_____
_____
_____
_____
_____
_____
_____
_____

Made in the USA
Monee, IL
20 May 2020

31535320R00079